Surrendered

31-DAY DEVOTIONAL

"AN INVITATION TO ALLOW GOD TO LEAD"

SHAUNA HARRISON

All scriptures are quoted from the KJV, NKJV, and NIV versions of the
Bible.

Book Project Management — Start Write Publish
contact@startwriteaway.com
Start Write Team
Editor: Dr. Gerald C. Simmons
Editorial Assistant: Jennifer Eiland
Layout Designer: Erica Smith
Front/Back Cover: Dionne Allen

ISBN: 978-1-7341491-0-4

Table of Contents

Dedication

This book is dedicated to my God and to my family:

To Father God, without you, I would be nothing. You rescued me. You fought for me, and today remain my Great Defender.

My mother, Elease Smith, and my father Joseph Smith, whose unconditional love, guidance & parenting has always been the wind beneath my wings and the wind in my sails. I could not have asked God for better parents.

To my husband, who provides me unwavering support with the kind of push that only he can give that spurs me on to more. And to my children, Brittany, Isaiah, Kellen, Daniel & Caleb, who are all my "whys." You are my heroes and my she-roe. I am honored to call you mine and honored to have been chosen by God to be yours.

Acknowledgments

To say that all of the glory belongs to God is an understatement.

I have to acknowledge that my God alone gets the glory and the praise for this devotional. It is divinely inspired and could not have been done without His pouring into me consistently. He is the reason for my existence. He has loved me with infinite love, and for that, I am grateful.

INTRODUCTION —
Surrendered ... to?

Surrender.

This word is probably one of the hardest words to fully embrace or understand because the act of being surrendered is difficult for most of us to wrap our brains around. Well, just think about it. We come out of the womb, usually, when we feel like it. However, some of us are forced; others of us keep expectant loved ones waiting for hours and sometimes days. As toddlers, we have built-in wills that cause any new mom or dad to scratch her or his head in confusion and ask, "How am I going to discipline this child?"

The desire to "surrender" to anything or anyone doesn't seem to get easier with time or age — without work. In fact, much of the world struggles with surrender and continues to chase an inner peace that seems elusive as a result.

Let's see what we can do to change that. This book is a guided journal to help you find your inner peace that, I believe, can be found only at the place called "surrender." Finding the place of surrender is yours only if you desire to seek it and commit to releasing and letting go of all things in your life that may be holding you back from reaching that next level.

Let me also share that being surrendered is about embracing where you are while reaching forward to the deepest desires and loftiest dreams that the Father has placed within you. Surrender had been one of the hardest things for me to reach — a place where I was meant to be okay with where I was but not to be satisfied or content enough to remain there forever. You see, I had to understand that regardless of where anyone else was or what anyone else was doing, I needed to have real conversations with Father God about who it was He had called and created me to be. I had to block out what the rest of the world was doing. The "rest of the world" included those closest to me, and their inclusion did not make my focus on the place called SURRENDER any easier for me.

Once I had decided that I wanted to fulfill and walk in the path that God meant for me to walk. I was ready. When I had decided that all I really wanted, more than anything, was to please my Creator, the One who had poured destiny into me and had fashioned me on His Potter's wheel from my conception, I was ready. And do you know what? God was waiting for me there.

"For what shall it profit a man, if he shall gain the whole world, and lose his own soul? Or what shall a man give in exchange for his soul?" (Matthew 8:36-37).

DAY 1 —
Wake Up ... Rise & Shine!

"Time to wake up, Shauna!" my mother would yell from the hallway outside my room door. "Wake up. It's time for school."

I shared a room with my two older sisters when I was growing up in Brooklyn, New York, and sleep was highly valued because of the small, close sleeping quarters, and our different schedules. If my oldest sister, Jocelyn was up late, I had to deal with the light that she needed to continue her studies, and vice versa, so when Mom called, I had to wipe the sleep out of my eyes and determine that I was getting up to start my day. I must confess that it wasn't always the waking up, which was the struggle, but the real struggle was in my becoming mobile — actually moving my body to do what I needed it to do. The real struggle was getting my feet onto the floor and into action. Now that feat required my brain being "all in!"

"Wake up." Paul tells the church at Corinth.

"Wake up from your drunken stupor, as is right, and do not go on sinning. For some, have no knowledge of God. I say this to your shame" (1 Corinthians 15:34).

There are so many things that are designed to lull the alert believer to sleep in today's culture. As a result, many are in a "drunken stupor" — but not drunk with alcohol. Many are drunk with the "spirits" of the world's culture. Lackadaisical, slothful, compromising, and like dripping water on a rock, they become more and more molded to the ways of the world, daily. Today... wake up. Today...you Rise. Today...it's a new day! Let's Go!

DAY 2 —
Face Time

Becoming prostrate is the position of power, and it always will be.

I find it interesting that repeatedly in the Bible, we see men of God on their faces and bowed down before the Great and Mighty God. In fact, many religions of the world require that worshipers worship their deity at a physically low level, putting their bodies in a position of surrender by bending or bowing during worship.

The Bible doesn't require us to necessarily bow low in our physical bodies but to have a heart that is so surrendered to Christ that when we go before Him, He sees us in a state of humility and meekness.

You may not even be able to get on your knees because of a debilitating ailment. But some of us can lie down before the Lord, and others can bow only their hearts in humble submission to the Father.

Whatever you do, be sure to have "face time" with your Father, daily.

Get your prayer time in today, but not while you're doing other things. Instead, do so in PRIVATE, ONE-ON-ONE time with Him. This kind of meeting is where your change comes. It is in the place of surrender, daily, that you learn to become transparent. It is in this place that chains will be broken, and your relationship with the Father can be nurtured and thereby catapulted to another level.

Schedule Him in your days until you get to the point where you can't live without seeing Him, hearing Him, being with Him. Daily.

> "Very early in the morning, while it was still dark, Jesus got up, left the house and went off to a solitary place, where he prayed" (Mark 1:35).

DAY 3 —
Separation

A time comes when a separation must take place.

Separate from the old. Separate from those things that no longer have any place in this season of your life. Some things in your life were once very powerful in their own right. They have served their purpose and should have been done away with by now, but somehow, they have found their way into the newness that you're now walking in.

How did that happen? Sometimes, we grow comfortable with things and people in our lives. In fact, we even grow comfortable with toxic people and things in our lives.

I once had a boyfriend who was so full of himself and so wounded within that he exhibited these traits in his sarcasm, in his hurtful words, hurtful behaviors, and degrading attitude toward me. I had to make the decision that he was not supposed to be a part of my present or my future. Reaching this decision took a lot of introspection and even repentance on my part.

Repentance was important for me because I knew that God had more for me; even so, I had made the conscious choice to go in a different direction — a direction that wasn't God's first choice for me.

Making a choice to separate myself from the world's ways and from the toxic lifestyle I had grown to find a strange comfort in was hard at first.

So, as you go through this season of separating yourself, I pray for your discernment so that you may know who your enemies are and who your friends are. I pray that God will grant you the wisdom to know who He sent and who the enemy sent and what their assignment is. Often, the ones the enemy sends will look as though they are a Godsend, but if you look closer and seek God's face about the relationship, God will reveal who and what is FOR YOU.

Separate.

2 Corinthians 6:17 says,

"Wherefore come out from among them, and be ye separate, saith the Lord, and touch not the unclean thing; and I will receive you."

DAY 4 —
You're the One!

Have you given up on your dreams? Don't give up on your DREAMS! I suspect that you didn't just TUCK them away — but that you have almost STOMPED THEM OUT and stuffed them in the basement of your yesterday. PULL THEM OUT! Pull out your dreams! The dreams and ambitions that you once had may be a distant memory, but as long as they are at least a MEMORY, they have life!

In Ezekiel chapter 37:1-14, God shows the prophet Ezekiel a vision of a valley of dry bones. These bones once had meat on them, blood flowing around them, life causing them to move, but are now dry, cracked, and dead. And just as Ezekiel was commanded to speak to the valley of dry bones and call them back to life, I speak to every dried up dream that once had life in your heart. I speak to every dead vision and ambition that the Spirit of God once stirred in you, and I call them all back to LIFE!

You're the only one who can walk out what God put in you, the way that He intended for you to walk it out! No one else can do it as you can! You're the ONE He called to do it. You're the ONE He gave the dreams to. You're the ONE He gave the passion to.

I DON'T CARE WHO TOLD YOU that you are not the one to do it; if you still have a burning inside to do it, YOU'RE THE ONE, Baby.

#Youretherightonebaby (Ezekiel 37:1-14).

DAY 5 —
The Hand I've Been Dealt

"Before I formed you in the womb, I knew you" (Jeremiah 1:5).

There are people in the world who are in desperate need of answers to problems that they think are a part of the hand they have been dealt.

Each of us is born into the world through the same biological process, but each has come into the world with a different set of cards.

Have you ever cried about "things" just not being fair? Have you ever looked across the street and wondered what neighbors did to get what they have or what they're doing to look the way they look? The questions can go on and on in our minds if we allow them to.

It's called "coveting" what another has. The 10 commandments warn against "coveting." In fact, it can be connected to that little green devil called "envy." Sometimes, we can get so caught up in our flesh that we can find ourselves in the depths of carnality, envying, and unthankfulness for where we are, or for what we have or for who we are. If we don't keep our minds "stayed on Christ," we can easily find ourselves outside of the "perfect peace" that He promises for those who do, (Isaiah 26:3).

Inside of this PEACE is a satisfaction that when basked in, causes a gratification to be a part of who we are, thus causing the worshipper in us to emerge and the Spirit of God to begin to enjoy a relationship with us.

I invite you to pray these same prayers that I'm praying for you today! I want you to know that God sees, knows, and wants you to try something a little different than what you have been doing and HOW you have been doing it.

My prayer for you today is that God will heal every hurt that you ALLOW Him to heal and that He will open your eyes to the TRUTH of His love and His ways. Finally, I pray that you, henceforth, will be obedient to Him and believe that what He says will work to fix your problems and circumstances. In Jesus' name, Amen.

DAY 6 —
Broken Ties

Many of you should have broken ties with people in your lives long ago, whether they are family, friends, or boy/girlfriends. You've refused — even though they have and continue to DIS-HONOR YOU & YOUR GOD. Because of that refusal, you are in a place of mental, emotional, and even spiritual "cloudiness" where nothing seems to be working out the way that it should.

Your relationship with God isn't progressing because of the dishonor you've allowed. You haven't corrected them. You haven't repented. Their pull on your life is slowly causing you to be drained. In fact, you no longer even have the desire to seek God the way that you once did. Cut ties today. It can be done lovingly; however, you should immediately discontinue this unhealthy relationship that was for an old season of your life.

If you wish never to be fully able to enter into the NEXT season of your life, continue just as you are going! The simple truth is that they may have had a certain purpose in your life for THAT TIME, THAT SEASON, THOSE YEARS, but if you're GROWING and ACTUALLY MOVING TO NEW LEVELS, often, God has new people for those levels.

The old relationships do not have to be thrown away. They need to be RECLASSIFIED. They may not have a true purpose in your life right now. In fact, when we stay in a season for too long, or with people, emotions or things way beyond the time that they have been assigned to us, or we have been assigned to them, we risk walking in a state of arrested development. Remaining in old seasons and lingering in past purposes can be detrimental to our future. Your future awaits you. Think of your future as a living, breathing entity that is connected to the heart of God and set into motion by Him-for you. Think of it as waiting for you to arrive. Think of your future as missing only one thing to fulfill what God created it for. That ONE thing is you. Without you, your future is just a thought. It is just an idea. So, break ties with the old, stale, over-used and out of season things, people, ideas, and lifestyles and reach toward what's ahead. It's a new day!

DAY 7 —
Identify

Liar. Drug Addict. Murderer. Harlot.

Which one of the above do you identify with?

As I read the Bible, there are so many of the characters that have a history of mistakes and less than desirable lifestyles.

Look at Rahab. So much can be said about this amazing woman who happens to find herself included in the lineage of Jesus Christ. However, the only thing most can remember about Rahab is that she was a Harlot.

I hate it when people want to continue to identify me by my past. I've committed countless sins, just like the rest of the world, but isn't it funny that there are always those who will highlight the ugliest of sins from our past that they can remember.

As I look at Rahab, there is so much to say about her, just as I am sure there are a million wonderful things to say about you, but five times, we hear her called "HARLOT" — almost every time her name is mentioned. Let us consider these facts about this remarkable woman.

Rahab was a Canaanite. Rahab protected and hid men of God. Rahab found her way to be included in the lineage of Jesus by marriage. Rahab was the grandmother of Jesse and the great grandmother of David. Out of all of these facts, and all we can remember is that she was a Harlot.

Therefore, remember this about yourself today: People will call you what they want to call you. They will remember you the way they choose to remember you. You have no control over that. What you can control is who you are today. Be the best version of yourself that you can be. Be the you that God intended for you to be. Wonderful, Peacemaker, Gifted, Loving, Talented, Honest, You.

" ... and they went, and came into a harlot's house, named Rahab, and lodged there" (Joshua 2:1).

DAY 8 —
Barrel o' Crabs

Sometimes, we get so caught up in making sure that we remind people that EVERYONE sins, that if we're not careful, we will find ourselves attempting to justify our own sin.

The term "barrel o' crabs" makes most of us think of the one or two people that we know who love to give people the reality check of "We're all in this thing together; where do you think you're going?" type of deal. This mindset I hear on the lips of so many today who like to remind the so-called "lofty-minded" or the ones who believe that "with Christ, all things are possible," that "everyone sins," that "everyone has to sin," and that "no one is perfect." This "catalog of sins" is a barrel o' crabs' mentality.

Are you the crab who insists upon pulling the other crabs back down into the barrel with you? Are you the one who doesn't really want more, but somehow, you've become sur-rounded by people who won't settle? It's time for a heart check.

We have to check our hearts (it's an individual thing) to make sure that our motives are pure because sin loves company.

Our prayer needs to be "Jesus, give me a pure heart."

Just because we may not be perfect as man sees "perfection," doesn't mean that we don't SPEAK THOSE THINGS THAT BE NOT OVER OURSELVES AND PUSH TOWARD PERFECTION or HOLINESS.

I have the feeling that you are of the same mindset that I am. I'm pushing, pressing, not through any power of my own, but by the power of the Holy Spirit to become more than I was yesterday. I'm pushing to be better than I was last week. I'm pushing harder to make sure that when I fall, as we all do, that I get up and wipe myself off.

Our prayer today is:

May I be more like Him. May I please Him. May I hate this flesh and love God more than any desire. In the Mighty name of Jesus, Amen.

Because it is written, "Be ye holy; for I am holy" (1 Peter 1:16).

DAY 9 —
Misfit

I want to encourage those of you that WERE & perhaps STILL ARE like me ... what the enemy wanted to deem as a '#MISFIT'.

I encourage you to embrace the term if you haven't quite accepted it yet.

You're different. You've observed people over the years, and you know that you're different from many others. You've called yourself a "misfit." You've labeled yourself a "misfit" based on the idea that you don't really fit in anywhere. You've tried this group and that group. You've joined this club and that club. You've jumped from church to church. You've jumped from man to man. You've jumped from woman to woman. Why did God create you the way that He did? Why don't you really fit in anywhere?

I was NEVER a part of ANYBODY'S IN CROWD. I'm sure there were some who looked from across the room and thought differently at some point in my life, but I was ALWAYS THE ODD GIRL OUT. Maybe you can relate:

- Too smart for the cool girls
- Too far on the other side of town for the smart, privileged Jewish kids I went to school with
- Too proper for some
- Too much of an athlete for others
- Too dark for the light-skinned group
- Too light for the dark-skinned group
- Too quiet for others.
- Too aloof for the down to earth
- Too down to earth for the aloof
- Too much of a "church girl" to most (while others didn't know what to think of my plaid kilts, tights, penny loafers, and cashmere/wool argyle sweaters)
- Too sheltered for the kids in the neighborhood where I grew up
- Too weird for my blood brothers and sisters

What happened to the little sister we bossed around? Why is she on her knees again by her bedside praying in a strange language, sobbing and crying out to God?

I'm still a misfit. It's caused me to spend countless hours IN HIS FACE, crying out. Learning about who He is. Getting to know Him for myself, learning how to pour out my soul to the LOVER OF MY SOUL, learning how to trust Him & love Him and be at peace in His presence when peace can be found in no one else or anyplace else on the planet.

EMBRACE YOUR UNIQUENESS. WATCH HOW YOU BEGIN TO SHINE as you keep your eyes on Father God, just as a small child keeps their eyes on their mother and their father for their next cues.

WHERE ARE THE MISFITS? Where DO YOU belong?

These questions are not new. Psychiatrists, preachers, friends, family, and even teachers have suggested that you look for your place on the inside of yourself. They are all wrong. You will find out who you are only in the face of your Father God. You will find yourself only in Him.

There is a place that you fit in, and God is going to begin to reveal to you just who you are because you've been asking and because He has some plans for your life that only you can fulfill. Let's Go.

"Even every one that is called by my name: for I have created him for my glory, I have formed him; yea, I have made him" (Isaiah 43:7).

DAY 10 —
More, Lord ... more

Sometimes, we can sound like Oliver in the Charles Dickens tale "Oliver Twist" when little Oliver asks ever so politely, "Please Sir, I want some more," after already having had the standard serving that all of the other children had had.

Every level requires greater sacrifice. Wanting more of God is a desire that I believe every true Christian ought to have. It is the heart of the Father that every human being would not only acknowledge Him and accept Him but that we would all have a deep longing in our hearts for a deeper relationship with Him. Too often, we find ourselves wanting more of what the Lord has to offer and less of what He has to say. Although God is loving, He is also just ("He executes justice for the orphan and the widow, and shows His love for the alien by giving him food and clothing. Deut.10:18), and this fact means that His love is everlasting. However, He will not allow His love to be taken for granted, stomped on, used, or abused.

So, as we want more and ask for more, we must remember that "the promises of the Lord are yes and amen" and that He has so much for us. We must also remember that God always has "requirements," so to speak, for living that we must fill. Each level that God brings us to doesn't come without sacrifice.

"Trust in the Lord with all thine heart, and lean not unto thine own understanding. In all thy ways acknowledge him, and he shall direct thy paths" (Proverbs 3:5-6).

DAY 11 —
State of Affairs

Listen, it doesn't matter what you do or say. Some people are just not meant to be what you think they should be in your life. They just may not be able to be what you need at this present time. They may not even be who God called to be at your side during your present state of affairs.

In Genesis 13, we see the relationship of Abraham, still called Abram at the time and his nephew, Lot. Both men of the same family, with the same lineage, found themselves at a fork in the road when a quarrel arises between them. It really doesn't even matter what the quarrel was about, but as a result of this quarrel, the two men split and went their separate ways. Genesis 13: 8-9 tells us, "So Abram said to Lot, "Let's not have any quarreling between you and me, or between your herders and mine, for we are close relatives. Is not the whole land before you? Let's part company. If you go to the left, I'll go to the right; if you go to the right, I'll go to the left" (Genesis 13:9 KJV).

Abram was wise in his older years and made the best decision he could have ever made for himself and his family. Sometimes you have to make the hard decisions, and lots of times, those hard decisions will include moving away from those closest to us! Once Abram and Lot parted ways, this is the conversation that the Lord God had with him; "The Lord said to Abram after Lot had parted from him, "Look around from where you are, to the north and south, to the east and west. All the land that you see I will give to you and your offspring forever. I will make your offspring like the dust of the earth, so that if anyone could count the dust, then your offspring could be counted. Go, walk through the length and breadth of the land, for I am giving it to you." (Genesis 13:14-17).

Abraham's decision changed the entire trajectory of his life and the generations that came after him and through his loins. So, he made not just a life-changing decision for himself, but for every child, grandchild, great-grandchild that comes after he and his wife, Sarah. These are the examples we want to follow in our lives!

Reconsider your present state of affairs. Some people will make the cut; others simply cannot. It may be a hard decision like Abraham's was, but if it is the right decision, go for it. LET'S GO!

"He that walketh with wise men shall be wise: but a companion of fools shall be destroyed" (Proverbs 13:20).

DAY 12 —
Who Are You Living For?

Today, impress God.

He is impressed by your heart and the condition of it. He is impressed by your pure worship. He is impressed by your surrender.

We are conditioned to look for approval from man. From an early age, we want our parents to be pleased with us. We also wanted our teachers to be impressed with what we can do and how well we can do it. We strive to be at the top of the class in all categories. We want recognition and accolades and awards that prove that we are impressive. As we grow older, we find ourselves wanting to impress whichever group we want to be a part of. We may want to be the best athlete or have the most stylish and expensive clothing. Or, as young adults, we want to be able to get into the best universities and make the most money. These desires don't go away. They are fueled and fed as we get older. Our society rewards who it deems most impressive today, but it also attempts to destroy that same "most impressive" person that it built up just a few short months or years ago.

Let's face it. I believe Paul said it best to the church at Galatia in the scripture below. Paul says in a nutshell that it is impossible to serve man and God. He eloquently states that we cannot seek man's approval while also seeking the approval of God. We have to choose.

"For am I now seeking the approval of man, or of God? Or am I trying to please man? If I were still trying to please man, I would not be a servant of Christ." Galatians 1:10 ESV

Let's go.

Our prayer today is:

Lord, give us a heart that reflects Yours. In Jesus' Name.

DAY 13 —
Climate Changer

Regardless of what is going on right now ... take charge of the situation. Next, be determined to set the atmosphere where you are. Take a moment when you walk into a room today and take the temperature of the room. One of the sure signs that you are becoming who you were created to be is your ability to not be moved by the negative energy others may create in a space. Too often, we allow others who may be dealing with negative attitudes or negativity in their lives to set their atmosphere in a shared space.

Some years ago, I decided that I was no longer that person. Holy Spirit spoke to me plainly and convicted me of sitting by and not bringing His evident presence into a space I had entered, but I stepped into it and allowed it to change my demeanor. I conformed. Instead of transforming the room with what I had on me, and in me, I conformed to the negative, heavy, and weighted energy that everyone else was sitting under. It was that day that I committed to the Lord, "Never again!

Never again will I conform to a room! I will bring the joy and positivity and anointing of the Holy Ghost with me, and I will change the weather wherever I go! In any room, in any building, in any home, in any church, in any city, in any state ... the Holy Spirit takes over when I arrive!"

Change the climate where you are. Make someone's day and smile. Say some kind words. Encourage your boss. Pray for a stranger. Bring the glory of God with you. Change the climate.

DAY 14 —
Yes & Amen

Remind Him of His promises.

In order for us to do this, we must KNOW His promises. Doesn't it make you giddy to know that our loving Father that gave His only begotten son for you and I also left us a "last will and testament" called the Bible, and it holds promises that are just for us?

His promises are in His word readily available for you to lay hold on to them. This is the season that you decide to walk in the promises of God and to believe that what He said He would do, He will do!

This is a new season! Walk out of your old season and walk into this new season of Purpose and Surrender! Every promise that He has for you is yours to embrace. Every promise is waiting to come to pass. Receive them!

The devil knows every promise that God has given to His children! However, his job is to kill, steal, and destroy everything that he can that pertains to you! That includes the delivery of your promises.

But I prophesy over you today that every promise that God has spoken over His children is being delivered to you right now in the mighty name of Jesus Christ of Nazareth! Every promise He gives His children is being delivered to you and will not be stopped, nor will it go off course. There is still HOPE. There is still promise.

> "For I know the thoughts that I think toward you, says the Lord, thoughts of peace and not of evil, to give you a future and a hope" (Jeremiah 29:11).

> "For all the promises of God in him are yea, and in him Amen, unto the glory of God by us" (2 Corinthians 1:20).

DAY 15 —
Victory!

The thing about LONELINESS is that if it's an issue for you now while you're single, it will try to be an issue for you when you get married. Being alone can be a blessing, or you can allow the enemy to make it feel like a sentence. Loneliness has been described as feeling empty, isolated, excluded, or left you. This tells us that feelings of loneliness are accompanied by emotions that, if not controlled, arrested, and submitted to God, can be dangerous.

Too often, newlyweds or those in a new relationship think that the burden of loneliness that they have carried can now be put on their spouse. No one can take the responsibility of wiping out the demonic influence in your life except for Jesus Christ!

Let's break the curse of "loneliness" and turn being alone into the blessing of what can be if we push into the presence of God. There is a place called "surrender" where there is no striving with the flesh for what it wants, but only surrendering what we have to the Father.

So, today, I encourage you to destroy loneliness at the root. Put the axe head to the root and kill this demon that attempts to destroy. I declare and decree that loneliness shall not be your portion, but peace, joy, love, and every good and perfect thing!

Embrace GOD. SURRENDER IT ALL.

DAY 16 —
More Like Him

Your flesh will always tell the real truth. The more time you spend with God — in His presence, fasting, praying, worshipping ... The less your flesh will act up ... the less ugly, nasty, carnal, fleshy you will be. #Isntthatwhatwewant?

The more time spent in His presence, fellowshipping with Him — fasting, reading, praying, worshiping, the more like Him you will be. Period. End of story.

Continue filling up on EVERYTHING else, and it will continue SHOWING UP IN YOU & ON YOU.

You become what you eat.
You eat through your eyes, your ears, your surroundings.

Fill up on HIM. Watch Him transform you. We fool no one but ourselves and maybe a few people who don't know any better.

"This, I say then, walk in the Spirit, and ye shall not fulfill the lust of the flesh" (Gal 5:16).

#BefilledwiththeSpirit

#BeledbytheSpirit

#WalkintheSpirit

DAY 17 —
Cry Out!

"Call upon me in the day of trouble: I will deliver thee,
and thou shalt glorify me" (Psalm 50:15).

I believe that we are once again in a season in which the need
for us to cry out unto God is at a peak. The Bible has Scripture
after Scripture about "crying out." Most often, this "crying out" is
a manner in which God would deliver a person or a people from
their enemies, from trouble, or from some set of calamities or
misfortunes that had resulted from disobedience. This method
is so familiar to me! I often feel like Paul as he addressed the
church at Rome when he laments, "Oh wretched man that I am,
who shall deliver me from the body of this death?" (Romans
7:24 KJV).

God has dealt so heavily with me regarding this position
of "crying" out to Him over the years, and the main thing that
continues to ring out to me is my being blessed to have a relationship with Him. He has reminded me that as I cry out for

myself, my loved ones, and my situations that seem so "unfair," I must remember to "cry out" for those who have no such relationship! I must remember to "get outside of myself" some days and carry the burden of prayer for the less fortunate in spirit who worship other gods and make obeisance to these gods out of obligation and out of ritual rather than out of love and adoration, as believers do for our Savior, the Lord Jesus Christ. Our hearts' cry must be for the social injustices and things that one may not call a social injustice, but we should be concerned about the things that are heavy on His heart, as revealed in scripture. It doesn't take long for one to begin to see the heart of the Father revealed through His last will and testament. Over and over again, we read scriptures like, Matthew 19:14 (KJV), "But Jesus said, suffer little children, and forbid them not, to come unto me: for of such is the kingdom of heaven." which immediately reminds us just how important children are to Him. Any cause that supports the well-being of children is to be lauded and certainly strikes high on the Father's heart. Or Isaiah 1:17, which gives us direction with such clarity; "Learn to do good; seek justice, correct oppression; bring justice to the fatherless, plead the widow's cause" (Isaiah 1:17 KJV).

Our burdens must reflect the concerns of His heart. He reminds me by His sweet Holy Spirit and by this scripture in Ezekiel 22: 29-30, that we cannot be carried away with our every pleasure and consumed with ourselves when we should be the "gap fillers" in the earth. Just as He said to the prophet Ezekiel, "The people of the land have used oppression, and exercised robbery, and have vexed the poor and needy: yes, they have oppressed the stranger wrongfully. I searched for a man among them who would build up the wall and stand in the gap before Me for the land so that I would not destroy it; but I found no one."

He says to those who will listen, today. We are the ones who have been assigned to fill the gap for those who don't obstinately cry out and for those who don't know how to cry out. I almost believe that the enemy that afflicts this earth and so much of humanity with the suffering that we see is looking on to see if we will, but for a moment, cry out and fill the gap for a nation that is in turmoil, and for a creation that must hear the gospel through us, and know the Creator in His love and majesty. Will we cry out? Will you cry out today for the one thing that God keeps bringing to our minds that we know needs prayer? Cry out for one set, subset, group, tribe, nationality, religion, country, a family of people other than your own who needs a "GAP FILLER" to stand in the gap for them.

And then may your personal prayer include these words:

"God put a fire on the inside of me that makes my heart CRY OUT for more of you! Holy Spirit, BURN in my BELLY like never before! Jesus, I surrender more of my life to you today than EVER, I surrender my thoughts, my desires, my prayer life. I will pray as You would have me pray, I will burn with a desire to please You and to serve You as I serve Your creation! May I be ardent for you. May I be a GOD-CHASER! In Jesus' name! Amen!

"Call unto me, and I will answer thee, and show thee great and mighty things, which thou knowest not" (Jeremiah 33:3).

DAY 18 —
Say It!

Say It As Though You Mean It!

"All I can do is pray at this point" is the confession that I hear so many people make when a situation seems to them as if they have done everything else to assist them for victory in their situation.

Please be reminded that the measure of faith with which we speak reveals the degree of faith that we have. If we aren't careful, what we say and how we say it is what we will manifest. I can't tell you how often I've heard this confession of despair in the direst of moments. Oh, I'm sure it wasn't meant to be a "confession" when it was spoken, but Matthew and Proverbs tell us that "out of the abundance of the heart, the mouth speaks." Our mouths reveal where we are on a matter. What we say too often tells the world how we really think, how we really feel, and how much faith we really have.

Great men and women of God, like Kenneth Hagin, Smith Wigglesworth, and Katherine Kuhlman, taught on faith with a vengeance that not many presently have. As a teenager and young adult, and even now, I find myself devouring teachings from some of these great teachers of faith! Spiritual Generals such as Apostle Frederick have been devoted to equipping the body of Christ on how to live by faith. I have binged for days listening and learning from this great man of God. Yet I have still found myself falling back to the way of my old man, which, in times of distress, can reach for solutions from everywhere other than my God, my Bible, my Truth.

Let me encourage you today to go to the next level and not waste time with toxic entities in your life, but reach for the promises of God. The promises of God give us every reason to trust Him FIRST, not last. The promises of God are guaranteed if we only believe. They should never be reached for last, but if we believe that He is Who He has shown Himself to be ... then all of us SHOULD PRAY and believe! BELIEVE! BELIEVE! BELIEVE!

I decree and declare that you will begin to walk as if you are in a season of victory! I decree and declare a shift in your thought processes and a shift in the words that are spoken from your mouth. In Jesus' name!

DAY 19 —
Surrender Yourself

The road of surrender is a road about which every believer makes decisions daily. It starts with deciding how much of our lives we will give to God. Daily, we decide how much of our day will be surrendered to Him.

What does surrender look like for you? Maybe it's deciding to go to bed earlier, so that you can get up earlier to spend time with God – listening – getting direction – praying – worshipping. Maybe it's making the conscious decision to surrender your attitude to God. Perhaps you have an attitude of dishonor or disrespect towards certain people, or maybe you are known for being really short-tempered and will curse someone out at the drop of a hat.

Surrender looks the same, yet so different for all of us because we each have a different starting point, a different frame of reference, and different desires, strengths, and weaknesses. We can each have the same initial intention, but discover upon looking deeper that true surrender will mean something entirely different for each of us. The journey will be a different journey; the highs and the lows will be different; the victories and defeats will be their own ... each unique. We often tell God one thing with full intentions, but our own desires and ambitions seem too often railroad our good intention.

How often have you told God that you want more of Him? I'm sure He's created an opportunity for you to run after that which you've said you want! You want Him! So, don't miss Him. Dig in, and do the thing that your flesh doesn't want to do. Your spirit man is crying out for you to get up and pray. Read that book of the Bible that you have been thinking about. Call that friend, and pray with her. Apologize to that person that you have not forgiven, and "drop" all of the charges.

Once you decide that nothing will get in the way of your next steps, this is where the rubber meets the road, and He sees if what you say you really mean. Were you just caught up in that moment of praise and worship -where hands are lifted up, and the lyrics are being sung in unison, and the room is filled with the palpable presence of God, and you just said words that you never meant to follow through with?

The enemy has attempted to make you look disingenuous to the Father. He has accused you of being less than faithful to the Father just as he has with every man and woman of God before you. He has told you that your integrity is on the line with the Father. But I prophesy to your situation today that the mouth of the accuser is being shut, NOW. I prophesy to your destiny and to your future that you will not be stopped. Your relationship with the Father will soar to another level. Your self-surrender will cause others to look in awe and cause them to run to the arms of Father God. Your life will be a living testament to the glory of God! Father God sees you. He loves you, and He's waiting.

"Humble yourselves, therefore, under the mighty hand of God so that at the proper time he may exalt you, casting all your anxieties on him, because he cares for you" (1 Peter 5:6).

DAY 20 —
Passion

Today is a new day, and it is a perfect day to remember the things that you are passionate about. The very thing you believe strongly about in LIFE, that one thing, or maybe it's two things that you just cannot keep silent about and need to address in your life. If you're like me, you have multiple things that you are passionate about and want to pursue each one thoroughly.

Maybe there is an area of this life that you feel no one is addressing properly or no one is talking about. Maybe it is an injustice that you don't see anyone standing up against. I believe that those are areas in which God would like to use you. I believe that God deposits pieces of His heart into ours at a pace and level over which only we have control. He will give us thoughts and desires and passions and callings, but we do not have to answer. We do not have to listen or obey. However, we should, because when we do, we can be sure that the Father will have His hands covering us in our endeavors.

Today, don't allow the mundane things in life to get in the way of taking steps toward that which God has placed in your heart. You are a piece of the puzzle. You are a part of the blueprint. Where you are passionate, I may not be. Where I am PASSIONATE, you may not be.

He will take each of us, and if we allow Him, HE WILL USE US IN SUCH A WAY THAT LIVES WILL BE CHANGED, AND #TRANSFORMED. More lives will be snatched out of the clutches of the enemy, and soldiers for the kingdom will be made. What makes you angry? What gets your attention? What gets under your skin? What brings you joy? What causes you to jump out of bed in the morning?

Run! Make the time to Go and Do It!

"For God is working in you, giving you the desire and the power to do what pleases him" (Philippians 2:13).

DAY 21 —
The Real Reality

Did you wake up today, thinking of something that doesn't seem to want to go away? Often, in my life, I have had things that weren't so pleasant always remind me of their existence. Out of Christ, we are taught that what we see is our reality, our only reality. But any in-depth study of the Word of God leads us to the truth that the real reality is what we cannot see with our natural eyes.

What you thought was permanent is only temporary. Scripture instructs us to look not at the things we can see with our natural eyes because they are temporary. Too often, we are fooled and misled to focus on the elements of the flesh, things that humanity says should worry us. The Bible clearly instructs us to cast our cares on Christ, meaning that we release ourselves from the worry of our issues and troubles, which we can see with our natural eyes and feel with our natural emotions.

We must first fully embrace this thing and walk it out just as God planned. Next, we must have faith enough to get outside ourselves and to trust that there is an alternate reality that God has already crafted and ordained for us. Honestly, the blood of Jesus has borne what we are carrying and worrying about today. So, we don't have to worry about that at all!

But, if we don't allow ourselves to trust, then we can find ourselves discouraged and off track. If we can, just for a moment at a time, remember that what we see, feel, taste, and experience is temporary and that there is a greater REALITY — an alternate reality if you will, yes — even here — Heaven on earth.

> "While we look not at the things which are seen, but at the things which are not seen: for the things which are seen are temporal; but the things which are not seen are eternal" (2 Cor. 4:18).

DAY 22 —
Who Did Hinder You?

"Ye did run well; who did hinder you that ye should not obey the truth?" Galatians 5:7

When a person realizes that he or she is his or her biggest hindrance, God can begin to move in his or her life. When a person realizes that he or she is his or her biggest competition, he or she will begin to reach new heights and to soar in areas they thought were insurmountable.

Too often, we are our own biggest critic, and we fail to be the biggest cheerleader in our own life. It's important to take daily steps toward victory by coming to grips with all of these thought processes and by using them as the building blocks toward that same victory.

Remember this today:

1. If you don't believe in yourself, it can be incredibly hard for others to get on board to believe in you. It's not impos-

sible, but it is so much more productive when two agree and then walk together. "How can two walk together, except they agree?" (Amos 3:3).

2. Your mind can be your worst enemy or your biggest ally. Paul reminds us in Romans that we should renew our minds with the Word of God. It is through this process that we begin to take on the mind of Christ and begin to live and think and become more of what the Apostle Paul calls "transformed by the renewing of your minds." When we come to Him, we most likely come with a mindset that has been conformed to the ways of this world. That same mindset often feeds us the opposite of what we need to succeed. Renew your mind with the word of God, and soar (Romans 12:1-2).

3. Take into consideration those you have around you. It is often said that we are like the five closest people to us. Who in your inner circle is influencing you most? You are most likely to have resembling habits and ideologies. We all need to make sure that we are discriminating about those we keep around us. Sometimes, that means doing an inventory of those people. Are they who you should be spending the most time with? Are they who you should be listening to the most? Are they bringing toxicity into your life? Have they stayed past their season?

"To every thing there is a season, and a time to every purpose under the heaven: A time to be born, and a time to die; a time to plant, and a time to pluck up that which is planted; A time to kill, and a time to heal; a time to break down, and a time to build up; A time to weep, and a time to laugh; a time to mourn, and a time to dance; A time to cast away stones, and a time to gather stones together; a time to embrace, and a time to refrain from embracing; A time to get, and a time to lose; a time to keep, and a time to cast away; A time to rend, and a time to sew; a time to keep silence, and a time to speak; A time to love, and a time to hate; a time of war, and a time of peace" (Ecclesiastes 3:1-8 (KJV).

DAY 23 —
What's He Saying to You?

My prayer for you today, my Love, is that you would take the time to get into a place — a secret place — your secret place, where you can hear Him and pay attention to what He has to say to you specifically.

As a child, I loved those special days when all of my siblings were gone, and I could have my mother's ear and attention entirely. I have to be honest: sometimes it was delightful, but there were other times when it wasn't the most pleasant because she might have had me cleaning, cooking, studying, or running errands of some sort. But on those days when I could just sit under her and with her as she moved about, those were some of the best days. She would talk and talk and talk about everything, and I just soaked it up. I don't think she ever realized how much I took away from just listening to her talk to me about what should be done and how, and why things should be done a certain way.

There were also days when my father would take my sister and me driving all over New York City and its boroughs. There was no telling where my father would be taking us if we decided to take him up on the offer of riding with him for the day. Those were some of the most eventful and exciting days! My father would take us on journeys all around Brooklyn, stop at stores that friends owned and car lots and garages that were owned by our family. We also stopped at different restaurants to eat. All the while, we were able to listen to his stories about the many adventures that he had. Those conversations with me, and those with friends or family while I listened on these "sacred" days were a privilege. It was as though I had been given for that day private moments, some jewels of knowledge, nuggets of wisdom, and even personal direction that had been saved just for me — just for when he or mom could get me alone. I imagine it was the same for my brothers and sisters. But somehow, it still made me feel so special.

This experience is what our lives should be like with the Father — what our relationships should resemble with Abba! And guess what? It was the Father Who gave us these ideas of what a parent/child relationship should look like! Humans didn't think of this on their own. We are made in the image of God, and we do what our Father has deposited in us. When you take the time to sit in the presence of Father God to love on Him, to know Him and to understand His ways and hear Him speak to us, is the beginning of a life-changing and transformational relationship in the making.

"He that dwelleth in the secret place of the most High shall abide under the shadow of the Almighty" (Psalm 91:1).

Declare this for yourself:

I declare in Jesus' name — in agreement with His word — that His words will bring healing to my whole body, spirit, and soul. In Jesus' name!

Let us go now to one of the "Wisdom" books:

"My child, pay attention to what I say. Listen carefully to my words. Don't lose sight of them. Let them penetrate deep into your heart, for they bring life to those who find them, and healing to their whole body" (Proverbs 4:20-22).

DAY 24 —
Cry Baby

This lesson may hit a little harder today. There is a Scripture that says, "When I was a child, I spake as a child, I understood as a child, but when I became a man, I put away childish things" (1 Corinthians 13:11).

We all start out in life as babies.

We also start this spiritual walk with Christ as what the Bible calls "babes in Christ," whom we, as Paul says, "should desire the sincere milk of the word 1 Peter 2:2. My parents were hardcore about developing a mature character in us. I realized later in life that while they were hardcore in helping us to mature and develop emotionally, mentally, and even spiritually. After I moved out and was on my own, it was now time for me to take responsibility to build my own character so that I could continue to "grow up" and become a valuable contributing member of society and the body of Christ. To accomplish this, we must cope with many different personality types. Additionally, we must interact with various types of people in a mature manner.

Two huge indicators of immaturity, especially spiritual immaturity, is that you may get offended very easily and no longer want to work with or deal with a person because of the offense. Or you may be emotionally unstable in many ways. Perhaps, you don't deal well with breakups, or are unable to be a good friend to anyone. Maybe you are unable to have healthy male/female platonic relationships because you think that they all have to end up with sexual interaction. People have to walk on eggshells around you, or someone says something and meant no harm at all; however, you judge him or her because it hit something in you. Rather than looking at yourself and asking, "Why did that offend me? How can I move higher in Christ, mature in this area so that I am not so easily put off my game?" Also, you want to point fingers at the person, and he or she may very well be wrong, but there isn't anything you can do about that. You can only address your own issues since you have power over you.

Maybe you've noticed that your feelings and emotions are all over the place and that you're double-minded and unable to control your emotions. What is more, you have mood swings. One day you're good; the next day you're not. These examples represent flesh in control, meaning that your flesh is in control. Your spirit man is very likely quite weak and needs to be strengthened so that the Holy Spirit may step in and help you to walk in Godly character.

But there is a timestamp and a time limit. There is an appointed time for you to begin to grow up and mature. God is waiting, and He believes in you. He is waiting to release parts of your inheritance once you make up your mind to shake off IMMATURITY and reach toward having a more mature mindset. There are things that He cannot trust you with until that time. Let's go.

"What I am saying is that as long as an heir is underage, he is no different from a slave, although he owns the whole estate. The heir is subject to guardians and trustees until the time set by his father" (Galatians 4:1-2).

"When I was a child, I spake as a child, I understood as a child, I thought as a child: but when I became a man, I put away childish things" (1 Cor. 13:11).

DAY 25 —
What's For Dinner?

You know that some things cannot be eaten regularly. You know what those things are for you — those things that are often so desirable to your palate that you crave them almost uncontrollably. But it may be those very things that are slowly killing you. The things that come to mind for me are things like bleached, white sugar, and many processed foods that we may enjoy but have chemicals that cause all sorts of sickness and disease over time. We may not see or feel the results of what taking these foods into our bodies is doing to us right away, but in time, ailments crop up, and we wonder where they came from. Frequently, people will see their physical bodies become weakened or compromised and wonder if the weakened condition is a result of their healthful diet.

Now, of course, the things that you are feeding your soul man may not be visibly killing you. However, what you feed yourself, let into your eye gates and your ear gates, determines just how strong you will be in this walk of faith with God;

therefore, we soon find ourselves thinking about those things, sounding like those things, and craving more of those things night after night and day after day. In today's television lineup for adults, we are likely to see items advertised on television that are so far from what any Christian should be eating. By watching shows that are filled with everything that you are trying to live holy from, you are sabotaging your own success.

By listening to music that doesn't feed you to build you up, strengthen you, or glorify your God, you potentially sabotage good Word of God seed that has been sown into your heart. This good seed was attempting to take root in the ground of your heart. The seed should bring forth a harvest that was meant to benefit you, and to all that you are connected. Therefore, consider your children and grandchildren.

I thank God that I know what I cannot eat or allow into my eye gates and ear gates. I didn't always know what was acceptable for me, much less that of anyone else. As I grew in Christ and began to seek Him for myself, the Holy Spirit began to convict me. Just as bad food eaten manifests itself in BAD ways in your body, so it is for food that we feed our souls. It will manifest if we don't uproot it and destroy it before it chokes out all of the good seed that has been sown.

An example of good stuff eaten = the WORD OF GOD — is good for the body/soul/spirit. An example of bad stuff eaten = SO MUCH OF TELEVISION, MOVIES, MUSIC, etc. that is clearly degrading, full of sin: sinful acts and speech that go against God — is horrible for the body/soul/spirit. So that's what I challenge you to press into today. I challenge you to start your day with the noble intention to eat only those things that will edify you, exhort you, and comfort you. I challenge you to allow into your space only those things that you would allow in if Jesus were standing right next to you because He is.

What do you want to manifest in your life in the not so distant future?

EAT IT.

"I will not set before my eyes anything that is worthless. I hate the work of those who fall away; it shall not cling to me" (Psalm 101:3).

"Your eye is the lamp of your body. When your eye is healthy, your whole body is full of light, but when it is bad, your body is full of darkness" (Luke 11:34).

"If your right eye causes you to sin, pluck it out and cast it from you; for it is more profitable for you that one of your members perish, than for your whole body to be cast into hell. And if your right hand causes you to sin, cut it off and cast it from you; for it is more profitable for you that one of your members perish, than for your whole body to be cast into hell" (Matt 5:29-30 NKJV).

#Eatitandbecomeit

DAY 26 —
It's Time

It's time to stop pushing the pain down. It's time to deal with it.

So much hurt and pain exist in the world. No matter where you go, you will always find people who are dealing with unhealed hurt or wounds that are still wide open. Hurting, wounded people are just an aspect of life. When Adam and Eve allowed sin to enter the picture, the first man and woman allowed a great deal to enter. I have to ask myself, "If they had only known the consequences, would they have?" I can imagine the first signs of being hurt when Cain slew Abel. I can't imagine the pain that murder and betrayal must have caused in the "first family." The pain Eve must have felt, and the hurt Adam experienced when his two prized accomplishments fought continuously until one's life was ended by the other is disturbing even today. Living in an imperfect world and muddied up by sin is what we can now call "the norm," unfortunately.

1 Peter 5 says that we should "Cast all of your care upon Him, because He cares for us." We need to grasp the fact that Jesus took our pain, our hurt, our offense — all of it — on the cross. If we allow Him to continue to carry it and keep it, Jesus will heal and restore and refresh and remake us as He does what He does best.

I'd like to share with you a few of the things that I know will help to bring a shift from pain to focusing on purpose.

1. Be honest with yourself about your feelings.

2. Don't lie about what you're feeling about the people and circumstances that hurt you.

3. Journal about it to God.

4. Talk about it to God, not to people who do not give Godly counsel.

5. Forgive. It is often a tedious process, but it must be done. Confess daily to yourself that you forgive the person/people who hurt you.

6. Pray for the person/people who hurt you.

7. Walk surrendered before God — every part of you.

8. Build your relationship with God through planned, consistent reading of your Bible and constant prayer.

    Casting all your care upon him; for He careth for you. (1 Peter 5:7).

"But Jesus said unto her, Let the children first be filled: for it is not meet to take the children's bread, and to cast it unto the dogs" (Mark 7:27).

And so, just as the Bible says, "Healing is the children's bread. Healing is yours, Deliverance is yours, Receive it.

DAY 27 —
Give Thanks

No matter where you see yourself today, thank God that He's done what He's done with you so far. It may not even be much in your eyes, but THANK HIM! Then, continue to let Him cut away, purge, and burn up the ugliness that you struggle with daily. YES, daily. It's TOO LATE in the day to act as though you don't have some ugly thought or practice that needs to be burned up in the refiner's fire … burn it up, Lord.

I encourage you to meditate on these scriptures:

"Give thanks to the Lord, for he is good; his love endures forever" (**1 Chronicles 16:34 NIV).**

"I will give thanks to you, Lord, with all my heart; I will tell of all your wonderful deeds" (**Psalm 9:1 NIV).**

"I will praise God's name in song and glorify him with thanksgiving" (**Psalm 69:30 NIV).**

"I will give thanks to you, Lord, with all my heart; I will

tell of all your wonderful deeds" **(Psalm 9:1 NIV).**

"Do not be anxious about anything, but in every situation, by prayer and petition, with thanksgiving, present your requests to God. And the peace of God, which transcends all understanding, will guard your hearts and your minds in Christ Jesus" **(Philippians 4:6-7 NIV).**

DAY 28 —
Glow Stick Christianity

You can't BE LIGHT and shine light if you don't have a LIGHT to shine.

So many people in America say that they are Christians. This is because we have, as a nation, believed and been founded on Judeo-Christian values. We have been seen around the world as a Christian nation for the most part, or at least, we were for many, many years. There was a time when if you came from a Christian family, you called yourself a Christian. I believe we still have those people right here in "good ole America." They say they were born Christians. They say they love Jesus. They say their whole family is Christian. They say they have not been to church in thirty years, but they are Christian.

Well, that is a different type of Christianity than what Jesus was pushing. That is different than what the church in Acts was selling. That kind of Christianity always gets mixed up with "my kind." "My kind" is the kind where I had an encounter. Yes, my parents called us Protestants when I was growing up. I didn't know what that really meant. But it was comforting to know what we were. Yeah, I had an encounter with Jesus that shook me to my core. It changed me from the inside out. It set a fire on the inside of me that almost made me look different on the outside and act differently when I went back to school after summer vacation. I told all of my closest friends that I had had an encounter with Christ, where He visited me, and I felt a love from His presence that was matchless. This Jesus that I had heard about, read about had become real to me in a split second just by me asking Him to be Lord of my life and telling Him that I needed Him, and I couldn't do "life" successfully on my own. I knew I was a sinner, needing His grace and mercy more than I needed the air that we breathe. This love exchange called "salvation" had to be told, it had to be shared, and they held me accountable whenever I got out of line. "You're supposed to saved. You shouldn't be doing that," they'd say.

You see, the kind of Christianity I had experienced and "found" had me shining this gigantic big bright light everywhere, even when I didn't want to shine it — in my house, with my siblings, at school, with my friends. It was the real light and still is.

But then there's this other little light that I have observed some carry. It is barely lit. It's often completely out. I call it "glowstick Christianity." It doesn't really produce a real light. It's sort of like the glowsticks that you get at a party, the ones that you pop and shake, and they last for the night, but when you go back to them, they are no longer working. They didn't have a good, long-lasting source to pull from. Not like this, "little light o' mine ... I'm 'gonna' let it shine" that never goes out. We may sometimes try to hide it "just because," or we may even see it getting dim at times because we have strayed away from the power source just a little.

So, take a look. Is your light the one that came from your family's bloodline of Christianity — American Christianity, or European Christianity, or wherever your family may have originated from? Or is your light a light that comes from the main source? Is it that light that no one can steal or talk you out of because it comes from the bloodline and from the blood of Jesus?

Some don't have the true light of Jesus Christ, which is why they blend in so well with the world and actually fit in quite well. They have no real light to shine into the darkness. All they ever really had was one of those GLOW STICKS that lasts only for a few hours. Perhaps what they had experienced was A false Christ? A feel-good moment? A child baptism that someone said he or she needed, but didn't produce light. A "holy communion" that the crowd was taking, so he or she went along? Maybe he or she went to church because "mom said so." Maybe he or she went through the motions and said a prayer, but had no repentance experience.

Those "lights" were imposters. Those were good intentions, but they had no POWER.

If you feel like any of the above are you, you can receive from the true LIGHT of the World, Jesus Christ, and be a light on a hill for a dark and dying world!

DAY 29 —
Entangled

Being a gossiper is such a nasty thing to be. The gossiper destroys reputations, but can only assist in destroying character if the "victim" gives in, steps down to his or her level, and tries to fight back.

The gossiper tears down, plants bad seeds about others and spreads garbage. The gossiper's mouth is a breeding ground for filth. When people see her or him, they're looking to see what filth will be spawned today. The wise woman turns away from the gossiper. She tempers what she allows into her heart because she knows if she lets it creep into her ears from the mouth of the gossiper, it will entangle her thoughts, and if meditated on, can seduce her with deception. She forgets that her ears are a part of her body, which she devoted as a living sacrifice unto God holy, acceptable. It was her reasonable service. She doesn't know that the same lips, the same tongue, the same hurt and the wounded person who brought her garbage to consume is now carrying new trash about her for the next person to consume. And the game of seduction, deception, and tale-bearing continues, taking out one victim after another.

LOOK closely. LISTEN closely. The gossiper births DEATH. You, birth life! There's no time for this madness. Let's Go.

Psalm 101:5 admonishes:

"Whoever slanders his neighbor secretly, I will destroy. Whoever has a haughty look and an arrogant heart I will not endure."

Ephesians 4:29 warns:

"Let no corrupting talk come out of your mouths, but only such as is good for building up, as fits the occasion, that it may give grace to those who hear."

James 1:26 corrects:

"If anyone thinks he is religious and does not bridle his tongue but deceives his heart, this person's religion is worthless."

Proverbs 6:16-19 informs:

"There are six things that the Lord hates, seven that are an abomination to him: haughty eyes, a lying tongue, and hands that shed innocent blood, a heart that devises wicked plans, feet that make haste to run to evil, a false witness who breathes out lies, and one who sows discord among brothers."

Never forget that gossiping blocks the hand of God's favor in your life!

DAY 30 —
Eat Well. Live Long.

There has to come a time in your adult life when one real-
izes that it's SO MUCH MORE WORTH IT to pay the price for
WHAT YOU PUT IN YOUR BODY THAN PUTTING ALL OF YOUR
MONEY into WHAT YOU PUT ON YOUR BODY.

We are responsible for being good stewards of our own
bodies given to us on loan so that we can actually make a difference in the earth, with healthy, well-taken care of bodies.
We cannot cover up with designer name-brand clothing what
we are not taking care of. Eat well. Eat good, healthful, God-cre-
ated food. Exercise, walk. Some movement helps as well. Just
Do It.

Make a difference in the earth. Don't shorten your life by
eating junk while "investing" in clothes and shoes that you really can't afford or that you really don't need. Hoping to cover
up with expensive name-brand clothing, the body that we don't
take good physical or spiritual care of is almost futile and gets

us nowhere. It leaves us still empty and searching. Once the expensive cover-ups come off, we are still faced with the reality of our raw selves.

I'm just saying that somebody needs to say it: There's a whole church world out there that is fat, unhealthy and dying. Some congregants love God and claim to be super-spiritual but refuse to discipline themselves enough to eat what God has created for them to eat. As people of God, we must do better than the last generation. They taught us so much but missed it in this category. We now have a generation of God's people who are looking for a miracle from God rather than looking to discipline themselves long enough to heal themselves through diet change and lifestyle change.

Leaving the earth prematurely can no longer be an option if we are going to fulfill the plans of God for our lives! We must commit to living our lives to the fullest! We must be challenged to walk differently and to let the Lord know that He can depend on us to take care of our bodies so that He may use us for as long as He needs to.

"Know ye not that your bodies are the members of Christ?" (1 Cor. 6:15a KJV).

DAY 31 —
Careful

Do you know who you are? Do you know what you're capable of? Do you not know that God has ordained that you be on the earth right now? Do you not know that you are not a mistake and that you are valuable to Father God?

Sometimes, we can get so caught up, caught up in what we see others doing. Social Media doesn't help one bit. Guided by it, we can get so caught up in comparing ourselves with what we see or believe we see others doing.

This preoccupation often causes **false feelings**. The reason that I call them **false feelings** is because they are based on incorrect information, which can leave us feeling neglected, rejected, jealous, etc., and not sure why. These are unhealthy emotions that the enemy tries to use against us if we don't control them. They cause us to focus so much on ourselves that we lose sight of the exact reason we do what we do or why we love as we love or live as we live.

Search your heart, and ask yourself why you feel neglected or rejected in a specific area or by a group of people. Ask yourself why you're so concerned with the elevation, promotion, or the attention that the next person is getting. This person's reward doesn't belittle you or negates your value.

YOU STILL COUNT. Celebrate the next person's victory without comparing yourself with him or her. You are your only competition. The Word of God must become your only measuring stick!

LET'S GO!

"For if any be a hearer of the word, and not a doer, he is like unto a man beholding his natural face in a glass: for he beholdeth himself, and goeth his way, and straightway forgetteth what manner of man he was" (James 1:23-24 KJV).

Surrendered Action Points

So often, we read books, and we walk away from the book with great delight and excitement about what was shared by the author, but we too often we fail to take meaningful steps after to continue the journey.

I'd like to use these next few pages to remind you of the name of the book by poking, prodding, and purposefully pushing you toward greater SURRENDER.

Over the next few hours or even days, do the exercises I have on the following page. Make a concerted effort to push yourself to have an attitude of surrender while working on the exercises. God sees the intentions of your heart, and He is a rewarder of those who diligently seek Him.

I believe that you picked up this book and read it because you know that there's more. You know there's more to this thing called Christianity and more to your relationship with Father God, and you're ready to be a God chaser. Right? Great! Let's get started!

Who are you trying to please in your life?

_____

1. Determine in your heart today that you will work to please God first, above all others.

2. Identify your passions. Do they line up with the word of God?

3. Move into the direction of your God-given passions.

4. Make a conscious effort to surrender your decisions to God before moving forward with a final plan.

5. Carve out a specific time each day that you will give fully and completely to the Lord.
   a. Worship.
   b. Meditate on specific scriptures.
   c. Pray.

6. Set aside time for yourself and practice self-care. This step allows you to tap into greatness and is critical for you to become all that God created you to be!

The above 6 Action Points are a few steps to keep front and center while becoming surrendered. Surrendering is a process. It is actually a moment by moment process that we each have to cooperate with as we become more like Christ consciously.

If you've found the above Action Steps useful, you'll love my upcoming accompaniment to the book that you're holding called, ***Surrendered: A Guided Journal***. Use both books together or individually. I believe that it will change your life and cause you to walk in the supernatural power of God.

Lightning Source UK Ltd.
Milton Keynes UK
UKHW022151270722
406484UK00010B/117